sonnets gives the impression both of fragments unified, and of a unified whole coming apart into pieces. These excellent poems worry at the world, questioning all its assumptions, trying every locked door and magic trick, whilst beset by interruptions of the poems' own making. In concise lines and flickering, mutable images, *sonnets* carries a real emotional freight.
— Martha Sprackland

A bleak, bloody, lonely and exquisite experience.
— Chrissy Williams

In Edward Doegar's preeminent lyric poetry for our times, the intersubjective and acoustic properties of lyric are used to make a kind of ethics of idiomatic address. In the crown of *sonnets*, he exploits the generic constraints of the eponymous form and breaks, bifurcates and folds its constituent parts into a different order, as though to reveal new dimensions in the very line itself. In a manner at once bracingly sharp and delicate, the poems render a violent moment of familial rupture and the contingent, contradictory meanings made in the aftermath, and the special position that poetry holds to make sense of it.
— Sam Buchan-Watts

A shocking act of violence is the catalyst for these sonnets which simultaneously interrogate both the 'wound' and 'stubborn doubt' of memory in a restlessly intelligent and hyper-lyric fashion. The vertical bar of these poems pervades and conversely suggests that in the dramatisation of division and pause, there can in fact be no division, no break with the past, no pause for breath.
– Richard Scott

sonnets

Edward Doegar is a poet and editor based in London.

Also by Edward Doegar

Adaptation (with Shakeeb Abu Hamdan)   (Kelder Press, 2021)

For Now   (clinic, 2017)

sonnets

Edward Doegar

Broken Sleep Books

ISBN: 978-1-915760-56-2

Cover designed by Aaron Kent

Edited and Typeset by Aaron Kent

Broken Sleep Books Ltd
Rhydwen
Talgarreg
Ceredigion
SA44 4HB

Broken Sleep Books Ltd
Fair View
St Georges Road
Cornwall
PL26 7YH

Contents

what happened | is happening again
in that this then there | of an event
recalled | so

carefully | the mind is obliged
to re- | cite the vision
witnessed | into rote

the tongue ties | that metal taste
to what | happened
sensing | my thoughts are

necessarily | bound
by the blood | in my mother's hair
that stiffens into | an accusation

I have long ignored | tainting
how | I see myself

I see myself | being seen
the impression | of a wound

the blood | in my mother's hair
that part of me | that I place

by memory | as one stroke
set against another | hardly

dry | drying hard
to fit | this form of words

grasping at | the subject
in hand | those brown curls

made black | wetly matted
crusting to a scab | that won't

heal | for days
livid | and still there

and still there | is this
lasting | that never before
and not after | of something
un- | understood

the idea | that I make
a problem of | the world
solving the un- | necessary
violence | by conceiving it

wrongly | what am I
trying to mean | this
for | I can't imagine
who could read this | just

as I want it read | as if
it happened | to someone else

to someone else | I worry
this must seem | too deliberate
too artfully staged | the sound

of a locked door | staying
shaken shut | that then
opens | because it must have

opened | so just like that
the mind | accommodates
its own | assumptions

the magic trick | is not
explained | as magic
or a trick | its paradox

maintained | maintains this
scene | I see

I see | an anger
acted upon | substantiated

into blood | the consequences
of feeling | felt

then unfelt | and unfelt
until | I can no longer

speak out | of experience
but knowing | that that cry

waits | somewhere
atrociously | sudden

like a stepped on | snail
without purpose | known

entirely present | in the present
of understanding | just how

just how | many lives are
justified | by so few words

means ending | in meaning
more than was | meant

as I've seen myself | seeing
tempers | what's heard

down that corridor | of becoming
I became | a stare

on the stairs | watching a scream
prized | from my mother's

fist-held head | sudden
and slowly | petrifying

into the mask | that wore
me | senseless

senseless | I must
be guessing | that memory
ruins | regardless of
who you know | you know
how they are | if at all only
as a perspective | borne
to diminish | the distance
so that here you are | me

in this instance | the sun
is in your eyes | the still
-light light | outside that
is a time | of day that is
a time of year | making it
so much worse | somehow

somehow | though
though | not exactly
then | appeases

though | becomes
before | and after
though | wouldn't

have | of course
though | though
must have | because

trying | though
unable | though
trying | not to

I blame | though
though | I can't

I can't | say if
it happened | precisely
how I | remember it
only | that it occurred

as I recall | no one
hurt her | as she made
a noise | I heard
but can't repeat | no one

drew | a gulp of blood
from her | hair
no one | raised their voice
above her | until

no one | left
no one | alone

alone | my thoughts
fascinate | in their own limits
with all those many | whites
that made | that sky grey

how | can I teach myself
to see red | for what
red is | allowing what it might
have been | to be what it was

something | then red and lastly
blood | understanding this
is not the same | as having
understood | as not having

the right word | is a form
of having | something to say

something to say | changes
into something | not discussed

alters | into what happened
and what didn't | the effects

that cause | the guessing
game | of who and how

to blame | the long lesson
drawn | to a collusion

of if | and then
getting used | to the consequence

of life | occurring
as an excuse | excused

by itself | the stubborn doubt
to be contained | in fact

in fact | falsely
displayed | my childhood
amended | by the past
tense | just as
surely | everyone else's
is | in part a part
of their own un- | doing
she becomes it | he becomes
did | and so what
must I do now | then
as now I hear | how
my words play | for time
trying truisms | such as life
as well as art | is a lie

is a lie | judged
by reasonable | doubt
rarely even | really

possible | or do I
falsify | these figures
adopting | hindsight's

clumsy | equivalence
when I tell | myself
what I think | I saw

and does it matter | more
to whom | it happens
or how | it occurs

to me now | as I think
the real her | bleeds

bleeds | became
bled | became unsaid
but seen | seeing
I hid | hiding from
myself | that knowing
that everyone | knew
or didn't | know
according to | if

it happened | again
I can't say | for certain
it did | or didn't
does | it matter now
how | would knowing
change | what happened

Acknowledgements

Thank you to everyone who saw these poems at an earlier stage and offered comments, encouragement and suggestions. I am grateful to Broken Sleep Books for publishing them.

LAY OUT YOUR | UNREST